Your Black Is Beautiful

George Earl Muhammad

Fulton Books
Meadville, PA

Published by Fulton Books 2022

ISBN 979-8-88505-689-2 (paperback)
ISBN 979-8-88505-690-8 (digital)

Printed in the United States of America

In dedication to my beautiful Black children—

Amarie Jackson,

Kahmyra Brown,

George Earl Muhammad Jr,

Kylan Muhammad, Carter Muhammad,

Jahcare Muhammad

and my wife, Aquila Muhammad.

I love you with all my heart.
Your black is beautiful.

Jamal
The Muslim Boy

Hello, my name is Jamal Muhammad, and I'm Muslim. I was told that because I'm Black, they would hate me and that because I'm Muslim, they wouldn't like me. Why would they hate me because of my color, Dad?

Well, son, you're not ugly. Your black is beautiful, so keep your head up high because one day, you're going to be important in this world. Your black is beautiful! Your black is beautiful.

Keyanna
The Christian Girl

Hey, Dad, I was at school today, and the children told me that the gap in my teeth was ugly. That hurt my feelings, Dad. They talked about how I was too light too be a Black girl too.

My Keyanna, your skin is beautiful. Honor it, cherish it, and respect it. You are an example of a Black queen, and your gap, in some countries, is a staple of true beauty.
Allow no one to remove your crown.
It was given to you at birth. My little angel, Black is beautiful.
Your black is beautiful.

Jason
The Albino Boy

Dad, why do I look like this? How can I be Black when I look White? And the children in my class make fun of my skin. The call me the boy with no color, and it hurts my feelings.

My son, God creates all shades of black. Your black is beautiful as well. Children make fun of things they don't understand. But you're one of a kind. Keep your head up and repeat after me.

Yes, sir, Dad!

My black is beautiful.
My black is beautiful.
My black is beautiful.
My black is beautiful.

Remember, Jason, no one can take your beauty away from you. Your black is beautiful.

George
The Colored Boy

Hey, George, why are you crying? What's wrong?

My friends outside are calling me the colored boy, and they don't want to play football with me. They called me ugly, Dad. I don't want to be Black anymore because I want my friends to like me!

George, look at me, son. I don't ever want to hear you say that again.
Your black is beautiful, and you are a king.
Love your skin.
George, most people talk about us because they don't see what we see. It's the difference between loving you and hating you.
Now let's play football, son!
Your black is beautiful.

Ini
The Jamaican Girl

Ini, I love your locks. I just love hair.

Thank you, Mama!

But Ini, why are you sad?

*The children on the playground tell me that my hair looks
nasty and that I need to go back to where I'm from.
They make fun of the way I talk, Mama, and I don't
want to go to the playground anymore.*

*Ini, in our culture, your locks are your strength. Your skin
color represents royalty in the Black community.
Don't allow anyone to make you hate your
own skin. Ini, you are beautiful.
Your black is beautiful.*

Pat
The Hood Girl

Pat, why are you out there, fighting?

Because Kathy told me that I was an ugly Black ghetto girl, and it hurt my feelings. I'm not going to let no one talk about me, Mama.

Pat, that's how they want you to act like. It's so they can call you out your name. So don't give in to them, baby girl.
Your skin is beautiful and a reflection of your culture.
Don't give in to what people say about you.
Rise above your emotions and embrace your Blackness.
It's the best part about you, Pat.
Your black is beautiful.

Ezekiel
The Rich Boy

Dad, I'm not accepted in my neighborhood by the
other rich children because I'm Black.
What's wrong with the way I look that makes
people not want to be around me?
Is my skin color that bad, Dad?

Son, money doesn't change how people feel about the color of your skin.
We've been hated on my people going on five hundred years.
Your Blackness is strength, and you are the original man.
So embrace who you are and the skin you bear.
You don't need to be accepted by anyone as long as you
accept yourself and who you are. That's what counts.
Your black is beautiful.

Savannah
The Poor Girl

*Hey, Black girl, you look dirty, and your shoes look very
old. We don't let poor people sit at the table with us.
Maybe if you were a different color, things would be
different, but you're cursed, poor Black girl.*

*Mom, they made fun of me today at school, and it really hurt my feelings.
Are we poor because we're Black, Mom?*

*Sometimes children repeat things that their parents say
about Black people. It's not true, but it still hurts. Your
Black is your beauty, Savannah, and it has nothing to
do with what skin color you were born with.
Rich or poor, you're still beautiful, Savannah; clothes and shoes
don't make you who you are. You are the original Black woman.
Things will get better, so let them keep talking.
Your black is beautiful.*

Jojo
The African Boy

Those clothes look weird on you, little Black boy.
Where are you from?
You need to go back there, and that stuff looks
like only something y'all folks would wear.

Mama what do they mean when they say "y'all folks"?
I thought all people were equal.

Jojo, your name in African culture means "God raises,"
so, son, you are a direct reflection of your creator.
Your Blackness is your crown. You are a king, and what we
wear is to protect our body while respecting our body.
They will make fun of what they don't know, Jojo.
So we must teach them about our culture so that
one day, they may under who we are, Jojo.
Your black is beautiful.

Layla
The Egyptian Girl

*You're not from this country, and I've never
seen a person as black as you.
What color of black is that?
How did you get over here? You must've come
in the night by ship or something.*

*Dad, it's wrong how they talk about my skin,
and I haven't done anything to them.
They say they are my friends, but all they do is make fun of me.
They told me that the color black is the ugliest color in the world.
That hurts. It makes me want to hate the skin I'm in, Dad.*

*Layla, you are a Black queen, and your Blackness is power.
That's why they hate you—because they know
we are the chosen people of God.
They don't like what they can't understand.
Always keep your head up high, Layla. Your name means
"Black beauty," and black is the best color in the world.
It's where all other colors originate from.
Your black is beautiful.*

Yara
The Puerto Rican Girl

Yara, you have a gap in your teeth, and your skin is in different colors.
You're Black and White, you look funny, and we don't want
you to play with us. You might give us what you have.
Stay away from us. We are not your friend.

Mom, what's wrong with me? Why am I changing colors?
They said they don't want to be my friend because I'm
Black and because I might give them what I have.

Yara, you're not contagious, baby. You just have a skin disease
called pigmentation, but that doesn't make you ugly.
Your black is beautiful, and your name means "strength" and "courage."
Sometimes we are born different. But God
accepts us all, and he loves you to.
Never allow anyone to make you dislike yourself or
your skin, baby. You are beauty at its finest.
Yara, you are worthy of all great things in life, so
embrace your skin whatever it turns out to be.
Your black is beautiful.

Kylan
The Boy with Speech Problems

*What are you saying, Kylan? You sound funny. Blah,
blah, blah. And I can't understand you.
I swear, Black people can't even talk.*

*Dad, do all Black people talk like me? Will they make
fun of me all my life because I talk like this?
Dad, can you fix me please? Can I change my color?
Will that fix me?*

*Son, you are perfect just the way you are, and your skin
color doesn't have anything to do with your disability.
Some people are just cruel and mean, but be
happy with your black skin, Kylan.
You are somebody, and you're going to do great things in life.
Smile. Don't allow people's words to hurt nor break you.
Your black is beautiful.*

It's okay to love your black, brown, bright, very black, albino, and all other shades and colors of black skin. Your black is beautiful, so enjoy your skin, little kings and queens.

Value yourself. Value your skin.

Be happy of your black skin.

Your black is beautiful.

The Black End

About the Author

A father of six and a brother of thirteen on his mother's side, George Earl Muhammad is a computer programmer with a heart of gold. George is from Chicago, Illinois. He has twelve certificates in coding. He is empowered by helping people and teaching others to know their worth and love themselves. George's dream is to reach out and help as many people as he is able to.